EDGE BOOKS

WAR MACHINES ASSAULT AMPHIBIAN VEHICLES

The AAVs

by Michael and Gladys Green

Capstone
press

Mankato, Minnesota

Edge Books are published by Capstone Press
151 Good Counsel Drive, P.O. Box 669, Mankato, Minnesota 56002
www.capstonepress.com

Library of Congress Cataloging-in-Publication Data
Green, Michael, 1952–
    Assault amphibian vehicles: the AAVs/by Michael and Gladys Green.
    p. cm.—(Edge Books. War machines)
    Summary: Describes the AAVP7A1 amphibious assault vehicle, including
its history, equipment, weapons, tactics, and future use with the United States
Marine Corps.
    Includes bibliographical references and index.
    ISBN 0-7368-2414-6
    1. AAVP7A1 (Tracked landing vehicle)—Juvenile literature. [1. AAVP7A1
(Tracked landing vehicle) 2. Armored vehicles, Military.] I. Green, Gladys, 1954–
II. Title. III. Series.
UG446.5.G68697 2004
623.8'256—dc22   2003016061

Editorial Credits
Matt Doeden, editor; Jason Knudson, designer; Jo Miller, photo researcher

**Capstone Press thanks Major Daryl G. Crane, USMC, for his help in preparing
this book.**

Photo Credits
Corbis, 6–7
DVIC, 27; Airman 1st Class Howard Baker, 5; PH2 Michael D. Degner, USN, 19;
    SSGT Cherie A. Thurlby, cover
Michael Green, 17, 22
Navy Photo by J02 John Harrington, 12
Photo by Ted Carlson/Fotodynamics, 14–15
Photo courtesy of General Dynamics Land Systems, 28
Photri-Microstock, 9
United Defense, L.P., 11
U.S. Marine Corps photo by Sergeant Kevin R. Reed, 21

1 2 3 4 5 6 09 08 07 06 05 04

Table of Contents

CHAPTER I

The AAV in Action

A fleet of U.S. Navy warships floats several miles off the coast of an enemy country. Nearby, several enemy soldiers watch the ships. The soldiers get ready to fire weapons at the fleet. Suddenly, a U.S. warplane streaks overhead. It drops several bombs. The soldiers dive for cover.

Seconds later, the enemy soldiers spot dozens of Marine Corps Assault Amphibian Vehicles (AAVs) coming through the water. At the same time, several Marine gunships fly overhead.

LEARN ABOUT:

An amphibious assault

Troop carriers

The LVT series

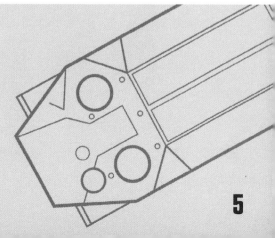

The AAVs reach the shore under the gunships' protection. They roll forward on tank-like tracks and drive toward the enemy base.

The enemy soldiers shoot at the AAVs. But their bullets bounce off the vehicles' armor. The AAV crews fire back with machine guns mounted to rotating turrets.

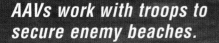

AAVs work with troops to secure enemy beaches.

A long ramp at the rear of one AAV drops down. Eighteen U.S. Marines jump out. Marines from the other AAVs quickly join them. The Marines rush forward and capture the enemy soldiers. The beach is safe for U.S. forces.

About the AAVP7AI

The AAVP7A1 is an amphibious armored personnel carrier. Its job is to carry U.S. Marines into combat over both land and water.

The AAV can move through water better than many other amphibious vehicles. Navy ships can drop an AAV into the water miles from shore. The vehicles can land in waves as high as 10 feet (3 meters). Most other amphibious vehicles can travel only on calm waterways, such as rivers or lakes.

Building the AAVP7AI

In the mid-1960s, Marine Corps officials wanted a new fleet of AAVs. Their old AAVs, called the Landing Vehicle Tracked-5 series (LVT5), were slow. In 1965, the Marine Corps asked the FMC Corporation to design and build a new fleet of AAVs.

From 1970 to 1974, the FMC Corporation built more than 1,000 AAVs. These vehicles included troop carriers called Landing Vehicle Tracked Personnel-7s (LVTP7s).

In the 1980s, the Marines upgraded the LVTP7. They renamed it the "Amphibious Assault Vehicle 7A1." The official name for the troop-carrying model became AAVP7A1.

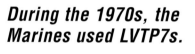

During the 1970s, the Marines used LVTP7s.

CHAPTER 2

Inside the AAV

The AAVP7A1 is a large vehicle. It measures 26 feet (7.9 meters) long; 10 feet, 9 inches (3.3 meters) wide; and 10 feet, 3 inches (3.1 meters) tall. The vehicle's size allows it to handle well in water. Smaller vehicles are easily tossed around by big waves. The AAVP7A1 is stable on both land and water.

The most important part of an AAV is its hull. This outside shell is covered with armor made of aluminum and steel. The armor protects the crew and passengers. It also protects the engine and electronic equipment inside. An armored turret rests on top of the hull. The AAV's weapons are mounted to the turret.

The outside shell of an AAV is called the hull.

LEARN ABOUT:

The hull

Water jet pumps

The crew

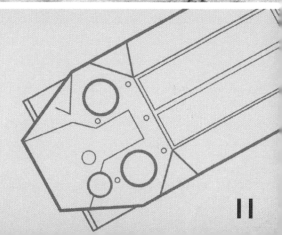

AAVs use powerful water pumps
to push through the water.

Engine

The AAV has a turbocharged diesel engine. This powerful engine sits inside the hull to the right of the AAV's driver.

The AAV's engine produces up to 525 horsepower. This power allows the vehicle to travel up to 45 miles (72 kilometers) per hour on land. An AAV can carry 171 gallons (647 liters) of diesel fuel in its tank. The fuel allows the vehicle to travel about 250 miles (400 kilometers).

The engine also provides power to the two water jet pumps that move the AAV through water. These pumps are mounted on the back of the hull. They can shoot 14,000 gallons (53,000 liters) of water each minute. The force of the moving water gives the AAV a top water speed of about 8 miles (13 kilometers) per hour.

The AAVP7A1

Function:	Amphibious Armored Personnel Carrier
Manufacturer:	United Defense
Date First Deployed:	1970
Length:	26 feet (7.9 meters)
Height:	10 feet, 3 inches (3.1 meters)
Width:	10 feet, 9 inches (3.3 meters)
Weight Fully Armed:	25 tons (22.7 metric tons)
Engine:	Cummins 525-horsepower turbocharged diesel
Top Land Speed:	45 miles (72 kilometers) per hour
Top Water Speed:	8 miles (13 kilometers) per hour
Range:	250 miles (400 kilometers)

1 Rear ramp

2 Tracks

3 Passenger compartment

4 Vehicle commander

5 Turret

6 Hull

7 Driver

S 53

Crew Positions

The AAVP7A1's crew includes a driver, an assistant driver, and a vehicle commander. Only men serve as AAV crew members. The U.S. military does not allow women to serve in combat roles.

The driver sits at the front of the vehicle. During combat, he closes an armored hatch. The driver looks out through a set of sights and instruments. Thermal sights detect heat to allow the driver to see well, even at night.

The assistant driver sits in the left rear seat in the troop compartment. In water, he watches for leaks and helps troops leave the vehicle during an emergency. On land, he helps troops enter and leave the vehicle.

The vehicle commander sits in the turret on the right side. During combat, he closes an armored hatch. He sees through sights mounted on the front of the turret.

Up to 18 Marines can ride in the AAV's passenger compartment.

The AAV can carry up to 18 Marines in its passenger compartment. They sit on long bench seats. The squad commander sits behind the driver. The passenger compartment includes two armored hatches. On land, Marines can open these hatches to fire weapons.

CHAPTER 3

Weapons and Tactics

The AAV is not a fighting vehicle. But it does have several powerful weapons systems. The vehicle commander controls and fires these weapons from the turret. The AAV's weapons cannot destroy heavily armored targets such as tanks. But they can damage unarmored vehicles and weapons.

LEARN ABOUT:

The Mk 19 grenade launcher

The M2 machine gun

AAV formations

19

Grenade Launcher

The AAV's most powerful weapon is an Mk19 automatic grenade launcher. This launcher is mounted to the turret. It can fire up to 375 rounds per minute. AAV crews rarely fire it at this setting. They use lower settings so they do not waste rounds.

The Mk19 can shoot at targets as far as 7,200 feet (2,200 meters) away. Shots at this range are not very accurate. The Mk19 can shoot accurately up to about 5,250 feet (1,600 meters).

The Mk19 can fire a variety of 40 mm rounds. The standard high-explosive round blows up on contact. It shoots small pieces of metal up to 15 feet (5 meters) out from where it explodes. Penetrating rounds are designed to go through armor. These rounds can blow through 2 inches (5 centimeters) of steel armor.

The Mk19 grenade launcher is mounted to the turret.

The AAV has a Browning M2 .50-caliber machine gun.

Machine Gun

The AAV's main gun is a Browning M2 .50-caliber machine gun. These guns have been in U.S. military service since the early 1930s. Since World War II (1939–1945), the M2 has been used in almost every Marine Corps and Army conflict.

The M2 can fire 550 rounds per minute. It also can fire one round at a time on its manual setting. The M2 has a top range of 4.2 miles (6.8 kilometers). But it is accurate only at about 1.3 miles (2 kilometers).

In recent years, improved armor has been added to many planes and vehicles. Machine gun fire can no longer damage tanks. But the M2 can still punch through light armor.

AAV Groups

AAVP7A1s usually travel in groups of 12, called platoons. Each platoon can move about 200 Marines. Platoons are divided into four sections of three vehicles.

Platoons may travel together to form an Assault Amphibian (AA) company. Each AA company includes three platoons of AAVs. A company also includes other AAVs designed for protection, maintenance, and support staff. AA companies usually have about 47 vehicles. Several AA companies may join to form an AA battalion.

The main job of an AAV platoon is to support Marines during combat. AAVs are not designed for direct combat with enemy tanks. Their large size makes them easy targets for enemy fire.

AAVs sometimes enter battles alongside Marine Corps tanks. They arrange themselves in formations. Formations include the line, echelon, and wedge.

AAV Formations

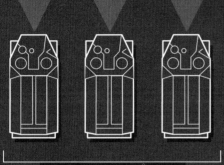

Line Formation

Echelon Formation

Wedge Formation

CHAPTER 4

The Future

The Marine Corps has updated its fleet of AAVs several times since the 1960s. But many Marines still believe AAVs are outdated. The vehicles are older than most of the crew members and troops that use them. The old vehicles also have become expensive to maintain.

The Marine Corps planned to replace the 7A1 series in the 1980s. They designed a new model called a Landing Vehicle Assault (LVA). Early designs showed that the LVA would be more expensive to build than current AAVs. It would not be much more useful. The Marine Corps canceled the project in 1985.

Many Marines believe the AAVP7A1 is outdated.

LEARN ABOUT:

Replacing the AAV

Building the EFV

EFV improvements

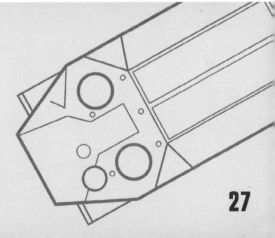

The EFV

In 1989, the Marine Corps again decided to replace its 7A1 series. They planned a new vehicle called the Advanced Amphibious Assault Vehicle (AAAV). The Marines wanted the AAAV to have a very high water speed, better armor, and more powerful weapons. The Marines later changed the name of the vehicle to Expeditionary Fighting Vehicle (EFV).

The plans to build the EFV moved very slowly. The Marines were unhappy with the early test models. In 2000, the General Dynamics company agreed to build a new prototype.

This new EFV model has performed well in tests. The Marine Corps and General Dynamics are planning to build more of these vehicles. They may build as many as 1,013.

The EFV will include several improvements over the 7A1 series. A powerful engine will allow it to travel up to 30 miles (48 kilometers) per hour through water. It will need less maintenance. It will include a powerful automatic cannon and a 7.62 mm machine gun.

The 7A1 series has been useful for the Marine Corps for almost 30 years. The EFV will help Marines keep a strong amphibious assault fleet for future missions.

The EFV is the Marine Corps' newest amphibious assault vehicle.

Glossary

battalion (buh-TAL-yun)—a group of assault amphibian companies that includes hundreds of vehicles

horsepower (HORSS-pou-ur)—a unit for measuring an engine's power

hull (HUHL)—the outside shell of a vehicle

platoon (pluh-TOON)—a group of tanks or vehicles that work together during battles and in training

prototype (PROH-tow-tipe)—a vehicle built to test a new design

track (TRAK)—a strip of steel covered with rubber padding; a track runs over the wheels of a tank or AAV.

turret (TUR-it)—a rotating structure on top of a tank or AAV that holds the main gun

Read More

Abramovitz, Melissa. *The U.S. Marine Corps at War.* On the Front Lines. Mankato, Minn.: Capstone Press, 2002.

Cooper, Jason. *U.S. Marine Corps.* Fighting Forces. Vero Beach, Fla.: Rourke, 2003.

Green, Michael, and Gladys Green. *Infantry Fighting Vehicles: The M2A2 Bradleys.* War Machines. Mankato, Minn.: Edge Books, 2004.

Useful Addresses

General Dynamics Land Systems
38500 Mound Road
Sterling Heights, MI 48310-3200

United Defense Ground Systems Division
P.O. Box 15512
York, PA 17405-1512

U.S. Marine Corps Headquarters
Division of Public Affairs
P.O. Box 1775
Washington, DC 20380-1775

Internet Sites

FactHound offers a safe, fun way to find Internet sites related to this book. All of the sites on FactHound have been researched by our staff.

Here's how:

1. Visit *www.facthound.com*
2. Type in this special code **0736824146** for age-appropriate sites. Or enter a search word related to this book for a more general search.
3. Click on the **Fetch It** button.

FactHound will fetch the best sites for you!

Index